- The book is based on a real-life time experience.
- The book is a Part-2.
- The purpose of the books is to spread the real words among people of all caste, creed or nationality.
- The book is not long like a story of nightingale or similar while these are the real sentences if cached by any individual could act as a catalyst to important purpose of life.
- Have a read and apply or visualize in real life.
- No Content has been marked on any human being specifically at all.
- All the content HAS BEEN WRITTEN AND is meaningful and purposeful for a truth seeker or content grasper or real reader.

Copyright Page:

# Understanding Spirtuality Scientifically

Spirtuality is not something that can be learned and stored information about. It is not like a data of exam or software which can be learnt or memorised or written down to keep it in a book or file.

It is biggest discovery for any human Being being alive through his curiosity,fortune,Karma`s and purity of actions. Spirtuality is something which can only be experienced with Lord`s Grace and Individual`s fortune, his inner –outer actions and the society n type of people ,knowledge,he/she follows.

Though there is no hard and fast rule that only certain individuals will experience and certain not. Anyone can have that chance in his/her life. But the reality of people who have been able to get that chance are people with actions to be able to impress Lord`s favourite disciples and Ultimatley Lord.

It is all within our inner self. Our Actions need to be self-less,true and in human deed. Our Existence on this planet Earth is because of the grace of creative power. If we follow World`s biggest space Agency. We can know that there is no such planet that Earth is . There has been no life discovered till date.

Science says that speed of sound is less than the speed of light . It has been proven with a scientific experiment and is easy to understand as well. The same principle lies in our withinself. The principle is to absorb the magical sound in the space of our mind and travel towards the light of origin.

Our Consciousness has come from a divine source which is administered by Lord and the soul has also come from a different source of its origin. Our soul has powers given by the lord. Such as we can see and listen.Further we have a face which has senses . The sense of vision,sense of hearing,sense of smell,sense of taste and sense of touch.

Unless one experience this or is not able to open Lord`s door. It becomes difficult to actually understand all these things as we have not seen Lord`s Place.

Our aim in Life should be to discover this one day or other.Then only the real purpose of life is complete.Time of every human being is limited. It can be 50-60 years,60-70 or 90-110-130 years.

Now Whatever we see on this Earth is false because number one it is destructive and number two is :Everything that is happening whether it`s World`s Biggest Business organisation running operations or A pizza shop selling Pizza`s is under the bar of Karma`s(Actions).It is under the acts of doing and observing .Doing and Observing means that the whole life we spent whether it is a life of Scientist,Doctor,worker or Actor ; It is all a learning and that learning needs to be applied in life to act better and discover truth.

To act better is not to keep on doing the same routine mistakes. Mistakes such as bad acts that actually devoid us from completing our life cycle. This Earth is called as a Holy-Workplace. If we see all of us , human beings are working day n night in one way or another. The work can be the biggest trade deal or just a normal cooking. We have to act better in each and every part of life no matter it is a small task or less money earning task or a very big earning deal.

Act better and there is chance of having fruits in life which again happens only with Lord`s Grace.When we act better we think that no-one has watched us but it is not true. Your better acts are always recognised with one fruit or another. We as human beings just sometimes lose hope and believe that we stop acting well because we want immediate results. We need to have patience and self belief that we will win one day. The win is over the bad times and bad happenings in our life.

Life is meant to enjoy. Anything we like we should accomplish but it should not lead to bad acts.

The little generous acts which makes us better will lead to peace and harmony in life. For instance if we observe relationship of men-women. The whole life women spents correcting her men and she stays worried a lot of times as well. While on the other hand men spend their life protecting the women and taking care of her.

Why we do all such things?Have we wondered ever? Why there is less individual life of men-women like men just do their own job the whole life and women do their own job.

It is natural attraction of living together  and learning from it which is a part of everyone`s life even for those who don`t get married. Those who don't get married they still talk and observe each other.

So the main thing out of this relationship is that it for us to learn about the relationship of our atma with the Lord.

At the end of life, A husband dies on its own and wife dies on its own. A husband cannot carry his wife to heaven nor the wife can do that.

So it is all part of falsehood to learn. That one day our soul needs to meet the Lord. As a matter of explanation husband-wife relationship is described as relation of atma n Paramatma.

We all are merely actors and players on this Earth.All the things we do has deep and real significance in life which we can understand only if someone Lord`s Disciple helps or Lord itself.

Our Time is limited ; whatever is in our destiny will complete by hook or crook. The weak part of ours is that we stop believing or again we want immediate results.

Rest we have increased our desires which puts burden on ourselves . Our Mind becomes desparate and we start feeling anxious.

# Who are We ???

Scientifically our front part of brain called as Frontal Lobes is where all the memory is stored. Our ability to think,intellect lies there.

Now with the energy which we see , Think and act is us. Other philospers said Because I can think I am.

It is actually The energy with which we See, Think and act is us. So we built our actions (Karma`s). We can see the dangers with use of eyes. We can act to situations .

We are the part of that creative energy . So with just a brain we cannot do this function . Brain is a organ for us which helps us to function the body.

We are the consciousness of Lord .So when we connect with Lord it is us who can drink the magical sound and connect with it. But the important thing to know is that we only become pure when we enter Lord`s Place.

And it is said when we are able to recognise ourselves purely then only we can meet Lord.

Lord actually meets us when we are in the purest form of ourselves.

We can come only in our purest form when we enter Lord`s Place and break the knot of `Atma and Mann`. We are the dot of Lord itself. That's why it is said `Asi Satnam Samundar de katre ha`.

Atma is billion times happier to enter the place of Lord from where she originated rather just taking cycles of birth n deaths.

Atma has the power to come back to his allotted body even after meeting and worshipping the Lord.

And when an individual accomplish this. Atma is less burdened of Karma`s and is in free state. As for understanding we say Atma is female and Paramatma is male. Atma is only happier and fulfilled of sorrows when she meets Paramatma.

The whole consciousness in the body is given to Atma for his journey on Earth. She has to complete the path of her journey.The good acts of being gives her the power to live with grace as she will not be in much of suffering.

The bad acts puts burden on her itself .We are the building blocks of Atma`s journey and we have a responsibility to follow principles and acts which makes her journey and our life better or say chance of making our living better.

We wish to have all the desires but not many can accomplish .The reason is our cycle of acts during the human time in different-2 bodies. But whenever we get a new body we have a new chance of acting better and having fruits.

So we should always aim to act Better just like we love to eat a Better Burger.

# Lord`s Cloud Technology

'This is an era of smart technology . People are using softwares more than hardwares such as we want to play games on a phone but may not be interested to fix any hardware issue itself. It is just a matter of liking software more than hardware technology.

Just like we love softwares we should know that we are all part of Lord`s Softwares as well.

Hardware is our human body and software is the Lord`s Technology.

And you should figure out by now that Why a lot of us like working among softwares or just say The Market is full of such great softwares in the world such as A Service app, A booking app and a A delivery app.

The idea here is to explain Why so many of us like working in cloud technology  and it is these days billion dollar market. Though we need to figure out that it is big falsehood to live in.

As we all should know that Earth is a holy work place and why  all the work we do is a big falsehood because The Lord`s Technology has designed it such a way that the activities u take part ; is a part of falsehood. It is not false as such if u  say Eating is false ; No eating is not false but the overall happenings and work done is a part of false hood.

And as a human being we will finish our life cycle through our actions one day. Our Actions if are pure,selfless and in human deed will solve many of our not only problems in life but also the further cycles and circumstances in life.

This is a use of term such as software and hardware through a way of explaining things.

Many People who accomplish Lord`s Path and meet him know this truth by heart. For others it is hard to believe as we need Lord`s grace to actually feel this truth.

Now many of us think that Why one person is richer than other person while he/she may have performed similar acts during his/her life?

This is also not in our hands.  People with better acts in life both previous and current reach farther but according to their desires and wants.

The desires and wants act as a wish which they may have wanted in previous life or wishing currently.

It is the Lord who fulfils your desires and even true dreams n wants. When we are fulfilling those dreams we never understand such things because we as a mind just believe because I do so I get.

It is actually under Lord`s Will such fulfilments gets completed flawlessly. Now  Because one can fulfill these desires for a certain period of time. That's The reason Lord`s Disciple`s preaching is important. It would be  our best time when we can love and meet Lord .Otherwise The Cycle of birth n deaths, desires n wants will keep on running .

We see how our environment is changing continuously . Already the life length of human being is said to be shortened due to many factors. There is no contradiction that Earth may be as fit to live as it is now or was; till next

4000 years or more but our time to meet Lord is limited.To finish the burden of cycles and ultimate purpose of being a human being . Though with current global warming trends and pollution it is hard to estimate the future time of all living beings.

Our Mind`s Activities are programmed that way and has effect of images it sees daily that it becomes hard to even believe that Our time is temporary and the purpose of human birth was some thing beyond our understanding.

For us to understand more about Lord`s Cloud and his software and his technology.We can take examples from current Cloud Technology we work in. The Amazing Cloud Technology which is currently worth of billions has all those things in it to understand.

Like we know Cloud has an Infrastructure,Platform and Users.

Similary our secondary souls are the users which help our primary soul (Atma) in the soulful work.Our mind has software to function during lifetime such a way that we can impress Lord.

The beauty has to be in our actions ; In computer Language it is input.The users are called helpers of this technology.

But never to forget not all users are friendly and not all are prominent like the customers in web services.Users keep on changing on our new human body depending on situations. They have lived in animal kingdom as well while also in different species. Users need to be addressed properly rather than creating a bluff in their activity is called as Human`s Mind Cruelty. Our Responsibility is to learn from users as well as teach what we feel is right and important.

Users play a big role in one individuals life. If users are happy it also means good news to big extent.If they are not happy we can act for better understanding about ourselves n show-seek faith.

But all in all our prime is our Atma which sits in front of our forehead. She is the power holder of all the creation .She though be using certain powers. She is the sub atomic creative particle of Lord which has true love for Lord. Lord has many creative and other particles which he can create and simultaneously use to get his play right as per his order.

For Instance when you see sports such as cricket: You see how everything is fast and running. The Speed and time of users in it is such that sometime an individual cannot match.To understand is that users are also the part of powers of lord to get his play done.He can at any time may place a new other particle at may be just on a empty chair and operate things n work done the way he wants. The Score he wants. The Sixes or boundaries he wants.Even the wickets he wants.

Users  acts always in a way Lord wants them to. And we just need to know that we are a part of this holy work place through the design of falsehood. We can never be truth unless we merge with him. And Everything happening around is to learn,understand and act accordingly for real purpose of life . Not that you start analysing this team won so he is the Lord`s favourite. The content related to sports is to understand.

On the Contrary,What happens is since we are so much indulged in heaviness of falsehood that we forget truth.And we also don't practice to find truth.Ultimately we end up having a mind which is largely in worries,insecurities,tensions.It is  not we don't have good times but we are actually mindful of other beings around. We always have process running in mind which calculates and compare. We also see each others scoring more n less . And we also start scoring more n less to secure places as well as accomplishing what we see. Such things to the mind`s level keeps on running and also our financial desires.

The others who are mindful of any mischievous activities that may take place: are mindful of frauds,lose of authority. The actual play is played by those only who are devoid of such mere comparisons and tensions of mind. They actually enjoy their part whatever it be.

To live that way Getting upto the practices of truth would solve many problems;Not your possesions .Your possesions definitely can give u more time but not internal peace that you will keep on searching until you are alive.Our time is limited so we should always wish to discover.

# Evolution

Look! Earth is one of the few planets that has Life. As per studies n investigation n experiments in this galaxy, Earth is so far the only planet to have life.

There is quite easy possibility that there may be another Galaxy of some other planets and it is far away and some other type of plasma energy ( such as blue aliens which we see in movies)creatures exist or not.

But what we should know is that Mars has no life. The Planet has existence which is great and helps many countries in their different-2 purposes of research as well.Similarly there are other planets Saturan, Uranus,Mercury,Venus,Jupiter,Neptune,pluto also doesnot have creatures . Many experiments or images can be seen online with a mere click that it is only on Earth there is life till date from say the times of billion years.

To figure out is Why the other planets do not have life while they revolve as well and are a part of galaxy.

In my view point Life has evolved from a cell and has made existence with grace of Lord`s Energy . Lord with his creative power has made existence of creature possible with his energy and powers . Biological reactions are beautiful if you believe in science and love the subjects of it.It was a cell which multiplied and creatures were formed according to their survival in the environment.

We also know that there was age of Dinosaurs but there is none these days.  One can say many new animals also formed depending on their cellular reactions and reproduction capabilities. Same is with human beings. We have evolved from one type of species which can be called as Apes,Monkeys n early humans.The Evolution was beautiful in its own way because we were surviving the habitat. So creatures were taking births and deaths depending on their survival capabilities in the temperature,wind,land,water around etc.

It is said that Lord took birth in the form of a human being . He lived as a human being through his formless energy which is in the space of our head. The subatomic creative particle which we can call Atma came from the magical sphere of light. It can be called as the ring of creative energy because with that energy life was able to exist. Atma was given energy and resources to take birth on Earth with a love inbuilt already through his technology in the space of our head to meet him during only human birth. To understand we use female and male nouns. She is here to complete her journey on earth until unless she meets up the lord .That is the reason when any fortunate one will take the help of magical sound to travel back through means of conscious energy which can only go back to Lord`s place not anywhere else: (Such as ;You cannot store it in a test tube or anything like a compound:) When a fortunate individual will get this chance , it is said he/she will reach to the atmosphere of Saints,Preachers  and will meet the Lord .

The Individual who accomplish will know the truth of space in the head .He will be able to recognise his true-self. He would understand that he was something else ,something very pure but was a part of dirt because he could not discover and practice this earlier.

He will have many benefits which are not explainable to practical needs of humans.In general their presence on earth would be fortune for others as they would have been able to connect with the creator of this planet. For more understanding Lord is the only creator of the Mother Earth.They will hold unique abilities to not only help other human beings but also many activities which can bring welfare.

Many great and famous people have accomplish such things in past and have transformed many people`s lives.You can take the examples of Guru nanak,Kabir,Buddha,Other Saints,etc and many.Their only presence has more power than others.

Their thoughts and words can bring more harmony in our life than others but again our minds are heavily indulged in loadful activities that it would be not easy to absorb harmony longer.

Our aim in life should be to understand Lord`s technology. Then we can understand more about our role and responsibilities. I mentioned previously that users may not be prominent and may not be friendly because users are also under influences also such as a human mind can be. Some are positive and some are negative influences. We have the mind and will power to decide right and wrong . Users don't have that will power. Your better actions can help you but definitely or not it can never be predicted.Positive user with more capabilities are more helpful than the opposite ones.

Life is a part n parcel of their activities as well. There is no way to get rid of bad users and deactivating them .They can be boon for one and may be bane for other. In modern technology ,User activity is something one can manage only with mind`s good abilities and effort to flourish.

Irony is that users are also part of one of those creativity of Lord which he uses as well to get his play done. We as humans has done many activities in the past which directly or indirectly affects user activity. Such as if We pollute our environment ; we are destroying nature.  In that pollution living creature may have innocent death which is not something Lord would want to see.

As in Evolution I mentioned Life did emerged through a cell but because this is Lord`s Place . For him every living being is important and almost every living being has his energy inbuilt but yes it is the Human Being`s life period in which we can worship and discover the Almighty`s Palace and be his fortunate individual. You cannot discover him in other species such as animals,birds,other creatures.He knows everything from your deeds to needs. That's why he is called LORD.

You would be wondering also that how do our Karma`s (actions) play part in type of next birth cycle. The way some humans can see or predict actions of other human beings. The same way Lord even without watching you knows the type of actions you did. He created this energy not you created him. It is his home from where Atma has emerged not you created it. That is why we are told by Saints that upon death Your Karma`s will be seen .You need to keep your karmic account better .

At the end I mentioned in my previous book as well that Whatever is meant to happen will happen . But yeah using the above knowledge and faith may bring us more happiness, betterment in life. We are a part of Lord`s creative energy as we can see, think and act. So we should aim to be a better human being rather than a normal one. If we try people have also reached to the topmost peak of mountains which is very dangerous though. So

Why can`t we reach the Lord`s place and settle our karmic account. Anyone or anything that diverts you to not believe in his powers and purposes of life is a negative believer or another negative influence which your mind may absorb.

## MY Thoughts on Karma

Karma to be defined is the actions taken by individual in a living body until his/her last breath. No individual is devoid of this artwork because he/she is born on this holy work place of lord.

People are actually not that aware that how this karma`s can be a powerful gift given to a human being. People are focussing on better life, better circumstances but they don't know why they do such things. Such as we want a good house, we a good life partner etc. All such things become meaningful more when an individual discovers this in his/her innerself that why he/she has been focussing the whole life on such things and wants. It is all to learn because one day or another by hook or crook an individual has to complete his life cycle. Those who are able to follow real worship and saints are able to have better circumstances and meanings to their life rather than those who forget the almighty. The theory of karma that is actions is all pure and one just need to be hopeful and believer that things can turn one day. There is no need to be scared of death at any stage of life but that should not be forgotten as well. Life is very short that is true but it is not that short that we cannot achieve real happiness and our real purpose of human birth.

When there was no culture of jobs or no culture of being rich with money. People used to believe jewls were money. People just used to work for the sake of help . Such as one man would get his camels or horses to transport things in exchange of grains etc. So time has evolved to human perception,acception and needs. Again if we like something we should do it but it should not lead to bad acts. So the current time of making money , being rich is not a bad idea. But all such things would have a limit and time. One will have leave the body for sure. Since that happens propotionally we don't want to take it seriously. So just try more and do those things which can help an individual to have better circumstances. All such things happen with better acts.

Every human being has a gift of human birth and karma`s. Karma can be your strength but it all depends on yourself. How much you can polish yourself. How much you can believe that your better acts will come back for your betterment one day.

People are indulged and don't give time to their self-understanding of the reality of human birth. Human birth is a gift in which one can achieve many things. Whether it is to the practical or mental needs.

It is all the play of Lord but people who have figured the truths of life can help other individuals in a better way.

They will tell you exactly what to follow and what to believe because the know how to tackle your mental  or practical needs.

If one individual is comfortable with the things he/she has and moving rightly to complete his basic needs. Then he/she will never be unhappy. He/she will have more smile than someone who he/she thinks is more happy.

So The idea here is to believe that whatever you are doing as your part in this holy workplace is your strength not your weakness. If you will cross the difficulties and will be effortful , then you should know that you will be blessed. So let Karma be your strength which is the first and foremost gift or step to achieve something on this workplace in a human being .

It is true that we are not told what was our previous birth that is not a right thing for any human being to know. As it can affect the individual badely to his mental level. So this is not a necessary thing to know.Nor an individual can be told his/her next birth as again it can affect our soul and individual badely to mental level. But what one should know is that it is the human being in which one can discover the truth of the creation. It is not possible in other creatures on this planet.

The idea is to love nature, support human welfare, tell each other a thing that can bring more prosperity whether it is jobs, financial security or ease of handling difficult situations. People who accomplishes right practices will definitely be Lord`s favourite and they will have better times. One need to conquer his mind to do better things in life. Don't waste your time in pulling each other down as good work have more power n strength than any such ordinary influences.

If we study a bit about brain functionality in normal and spiritual world, One can have a good idea of how things  works in spiritual world. The way there is lobes in your brain all of which has major function to run body routine mechanisms in a good manner. But different lobes has different function. The frontal part has a slightly differently than mid lobes and other lobes which are located at different regions.

For more knowledge and understanding , there is scientific basic information of lobes in ur brain:

The **occipital lobe** is the visual processing center of the brain containing most of the anatomical region of the visual cortex. These are specialixed for different visual tasks, such as visuospatial processing, color differentiation, and motion perception.

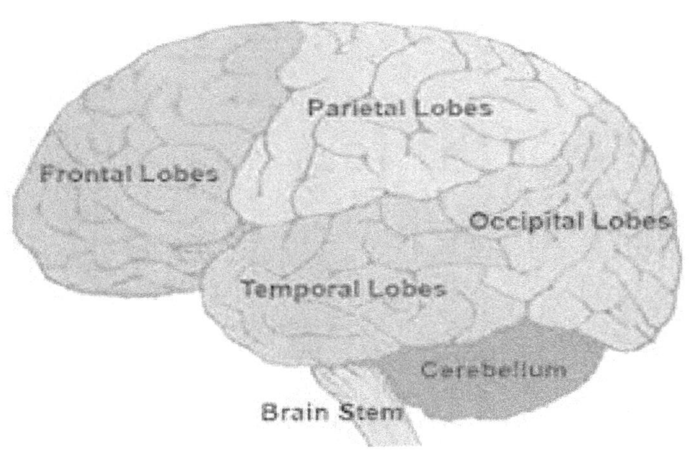


The **parietal lobe** is one of the major **lobes** in the brain,  is at the upper back area in the skull. It processes sensory information it receives from the outside world, mainly relating to touch, taste, and temperature.

Damage to the **parietal lobe** may lead to dysfunction in the senses

The **frontal lobe** is the part of the brain that controls important cognitive skills in humans, such as emotional understanding, problem solving, memory, language, judgment, sexual behaviours'. It is, in essence of our personality and our ability to communicate

The **temporal lobe** is one of the four major **lobes** of the cerebral cortex. It is the lower **lobe** of the cortex, sitting close to ear level within the skull. The **temporal lobe** is largely responsible for creating and preserving both conscious and long-term memory.

The **cerebellum**;This part of the brain is responsible for coordinating voluntary movements. It is also responsible for a number of functions including motor skills such as balance, coordination, and posture.

The user of any human largely sits at occipital lobes. So they catch and absorbs images more than any part of the creative energy we have. Here you can try a strong quote which is Seeing is believing. So the more one person indulges himself to atmosphere of saints, religious places, It helps user understanding and activity to follow practices required to meet almighty. It helps to follow those small routines that will bring us near to this grace n power.

## TIME

In normal world of living , people calculate time and it is mentioned in number of days, months, years or hours. But in spiritual world Time has different meaning to its existence.Time could be defined as something that is bound to happen and has been applied by natural power of this creation of world.

The same way in your mental space of head. Your Atma as a primary particle of Lord has different role.Your user which is secondary has different role and you yourself  in that space of head has  a role as well. The questions is how can the role be different or why it should be differentiated. See the way we can see with our eyes that this is blue colour or the other is orange colour.The same way Lord can see your primary particle which is his own created energy. Now the same way he can see us as all are part of that power with which can see,think and act with the help of brain. So to differentiate these three parts of energy in space of mind is not a easy task to differentiate because we need his grace to have that self -realisation.

The important thing out of this information is that Lord knows very accurately that which part of energy is acting and what type of activity that part of energy is acting and what type of activity that part of energy has done. It all happens very fast and is accountable to our account of actions.If user acts then user will responsible for bad acts and will face a push down to lower births species  . If we act bad using our mind/mann then we will face the result of it accordingly. If our atma acts bad or is not able to do good acts then she will also face. The user , atma is replaceable because they can be differentiated the same way we can differentiate colours.

The account of actions is called as your Karmic Account which the Lord gifted you when he gave you birth in your human birth. Now a mind may ask how can this happen? There are so many human beings on this earth. How can our karma`s be seen. The reality is even a single intentional extra spoon of sugar is also accounted. However we are naturally created to be very pure and generally act in good manner. But since the net of negative energy and aura of unawareness to level of space of mind is heavy on us that we cannot realise the purity of our own actions.

We can only realise the purity of our own action when we travel upwards using our only source that is God gifted conscious energy or body. In spiritual world the whole conscious energy is the body of atma. Atma being the face of it and the energy being the legs,hands and feets of it. Without This energy we can never feel the power of almighty and his grace without this spiritual practice which is mentioned in each and every religion of the world.

Lord has given your mind a ability of intellect .Intellect is your natural understanding of things. If we you would talk to two or three human beings, You would realise that not every human has the same intellect. There is always little bit difference (whether it is 1% or 99% )in intellectual understanding in billions of human beings at the same time . And it could be a  same topic .It is because everyone`s mind understanding is different and the energy in space of mind can help you to relate but can never be same because of dfifferent-2 karma`s done. So that is the reason people on this path are told to discover. That is also one major reason everything in this world is relative. Even if your highly knowledable but that is also relative. So no one is bigger than the other and can never be on this holy-workplace. If you have a nice car then there also millions other also who have a nice vehicle. Everything is relative in this world until your last breath. So if Lord or his energy doesnot exist ; there would have been fixed things . Such as no karma`s and no relativity. However Lord is not biased. Whatever you get is based on your first and foremost power . The power is to be able to act on this stage and be in human deed,welfare .It is just by the grace of almighty many difficult tasks are being accomplished.

The whole theory is to help you move to better acts and to let your mind know how it affects you practically and mentally in day to day life . If you will believe in this and will act accordingly and do small efforts. Then that day is not far when by hook or crook many of your needs can be fulfilled easily and flawlessly.

The timing of fulfilment need not be focused because you might be already getting needs and atmosphere . But you may not be aware as you have not connected with almighty or did not even try to. You are may be just attracted to a completely opposite work acts which has nothing but if performed under influences will give you sorrows in your later life. The good thing for us if that the part of energy of us such as user or us ; whichever part will act will be responsible for their acts. No one can run away from results of bad and good acts as it is getting stored and is immortal . To get up from bad acts and negative influences (especially users) is to open the Lord`s door with steps told in holy books ,religions and true practicer etc.

Lord loves everyone equally whether it is us,user and the pure particle of lord that is on mother earth .Lord also knows that every individual is almost on a test and journey. The test can be passed easily with just better acts.

People`s mind questions a lot and can say we have been acting fairly and have done many actions in human welfare as much they can.

Those actions done on this stage has power. Such actions always gets recognised. In human birth it is not all the days you live in sorrows  . but it is also not all the days we can be happy. So it is the laws of nature and Lord`s energy. It is his way to giving us things and fulfilling needs. For him it is beautiful to see humans loving humans. He is happy that we on this stage acted faithfully, saw his world and creation. He knows we have limited time but he fulfils many needs. Users are actually a very big help for any human. But the unhealthy influences and wrong practices. The urge to get things done very fast by users is sometimes bad for human health. Our atma helps us from negative influences of users and helps to keeps us on right path.

So The creators place is very beautiful . It is just we need to connect so that we can be more aware about his law and order. He showers us with those eyes to be able to see his beautiful creation.

And He is such a giver that even due to some circumstances if we acted faithfully on this stage but couldnot connect with him by means of spiritual steps.He stills helps us.But only if we acted better on this stage. It doesnot happen that a human keeps on doing bad things and say he was not aware. The time period of a single human being is not that short that he cannot connect or follow practices that is going to bring him welfare and peace back.

Overall each and every activity is a part of false design to learn and act better on this stage.

We can say that we learn about such things slowly but yes it is not that hard to follow .It is not that hard to understand Why this is false and how should I manage my time for my own better future.

Time will play a big role. Nothing happens before time. Secondly it is also in creators hands what he wants to do. We have the power of Karma and with powerful karma`s living better than in troubles. You must try to learn real depth of the creation or must try at least. Users and our atma knows everything because they emerged from Lord`s power and house. It is we who are unaware .But we have the will power to make it happen. User with right practices can help but they cannot worship for a human being.

Lord is a  help. He helps billions and will always help. We should just try to keep faith and stay in whatever atmosphere we get or are gifted with. The message is that The Karma`s can be your power than a burden or a load .